VICTORIOUS

Moving From Victim to Victor by Faith

Written By

Joy Regulus

In loving memory of George Moore, and Yvonne Crutcher.

To Jordan, Jaden, and Landen, you all are my reason for breathing. Thank you for giving me purpose.

CONTENTS

Introduction

Many people suffer in silence, from years of trauma due to childhood sexual abuse. I was one of those individuals. I felt alone, ashamed, and afraid to tell my story in fear of being judged or hurting others.

The silence and shame wreaked havoc on my life in the areas of relationships, personal, and spiritual growth. I struggled for many years to release the victim mindset which kept me bound, and to unleash the victor that God created me to be. By investing in my personal and spiritual growth, I was able to overcome the negativity of my past, learn to forgive so I could move forward, and to give thanks for everything I experienced in life.

If you have ever experienced painful events in your past and struggled to move forward with life, this book is for you!

In this book, I share intimate details of my personal life to help other survivors of childhood sexual abuse and other traumatic situations to know that they are not alone. Your past does not define you, but everything from your past will mold you into the victorious woman you are destined to be.

If you have been living a life that is less than God's

1

best for you, my eight practical and proven tips will help you on your road to victory. You will learn the process of forgiving; how to speak positivity and favor over yourself and your children through faith confessions; how to implement personal development strategies into your everyday life; how to connect with your Creator in a meaningful way; the role of health and fitness in your success; how giving will bring you joy; and what steps to take to write your vision for your life.

This book is for people who:

- Want to get over a painful past
- Struggle with knowing how to forgive
- Believe God has abandoned them
- Wish to help others who suffered from a traumatic past
- Experienced the loss of loved ones
- Lost a job or income to support their family
- Desire to chase after the desires of their heart
- Require more from life
- Need direction
- Experienced failed relationships and/or divorce
- Parented a child with substance abuse/addiction problems

Women survivors of a traumatic life have been experiencing victory through the methods outlined in this book via private and group coaching facilitated by me, and now this resource is available to help even more people.

writes: Kreslyn, a 39-year-old mother, wife, and client

I can't say enough about Joy Regulus. She came into my life when I was on the fence with what to do about my health. She has coached me through getting my health on track with proper nutrition and fitness...Joy is my friend, wellness coach, and my life coach...she helped me identify where my fear and self doubt stemmed from...I know that I can be afraid but I can move forward with that same fear and not allow it to stop me and hold me back...I have learned so much from this woman and I love her with all my heart...I am a different person now than I was a year ago because of Joy. She introduced GOD back into my life. I didn't pray as I knew I should, I didn't eat as I should, she introduced me to personal development, and I realized that I can love myself regardless of my size. JOY, YOU ARE MY ANGEL! I thank God for sending you to me and for you being obedient in living out your purpose to help women like me who need support to better themselves.

I promise that if you implement the eight tips outlined in this book, your life will change for the better, your joy will increase exponentially, and you will be closer to experiencing the VICTORIOUS life God has planned for you.

Don't waste another second living the life of a victim in pity and self-doubt. Take charge of your life and begin creating the freedom you desire today. Change happens gradually, but it cannot begin without you taking the first step. Victory is on the other side of your limiting beliefs, and you can achieve it by implementing the ideas taught in this book.

The life changing tips you are about to read in this book are guaranteed to set you on a path of freedom and victory over your past. Nothing in your life will be wasted when you begin to implement these tips, and witness the changes God will cause to take place as you step out in faith. The world is waiting to experience your greatness. Don't allow fear to hold you back one second longer!

Chapter 1 - When Life Happens

There is no chance, no destiny, no fate, that can hinder or control the firm resolve of a determined soul.

--ELLA WHEELER WILCOX

At an early age I learned that life is not always fair. I grew up in a single-parent home with my Mom and two sisters. I was the baby girl of the family; both of my sisters were 10 and 12 years older than me. My Mom was a hard worker and devoted much of her time to being a provider for us. She had grown up in a dysfunctional home with an abusive, alcoholic father. Most of her relationships after leaving home were founded on the principle of finding a "father figure" to take the place of the one she felt she never had. Unfortunately, this shaky foundation led to many failed relationships and all three of her girls being abused in some way.

I was no exception. My first experience with sexual abuse came from my mother's second husband, but the abuse actually began while they were still dating. Somewhere between the ages of four to five years old, this grown man took an interest in me. I can still remember the very first encounter very vividly.

It was the Fourth of July. We lived in a small studio apartment here in Huntsville, Alabama with one bed, one sofa, a very small kitchen, and one bathroom. I had fallen asleep and woken up that evening to find my mother gone. She left me home alone with her then boyfriend while she visited his sister to watch fireworks.

Sonny and I had grown close during the time Mom and him dated, so it wasn't uncommon for us to be alone together. His family owned a barn and had many horses. I enjoyed spending lots of time with him and his family there. I trusted him and looked up to him, just as my mother did. However, on this particular night, all of my trust would be broken.

When I woke up from napping, my stomach was hurting, so I told Sonny that I wasn't feeling well. He gave me Pepto-Bismol to settle my stomach and asked me if I would like for him to rub my tummy to help it feel better. I agreed. I laid in bed beside him while he rubbed my belly and felt as his hands shifted lower and lower until they were eventually in my panties. I was confused and didn't really understand what was happening. No one had ever touched me in this way, and I wasn't sure if he should be doing this or not, but I never said a word.

Fondling turned into him pulling his penis out and trying to penetrate me; however, I was too small for it to fit. He never tried that again, but it didn't stop him from fondling me any chance he had. Times when Mom was in the shower or away at church were prime times for him to catch a feel. Eventually he was brave enough to molest me in the same bed with my mother while she slept, and she never suspected a thing.

For whatever reason, I never said a word. I'm not sure if I was afraid or more ashamed at what others would think of me. At times I would cry and want to tell someone, but I wasn't sure who to tell.

Sonny and Mom married on Sunday, December 1st; I don't know the year, but I will never forget that day. It was the saddest day of my life. I was a flower girl in their wedding. Throughout the entire ceremony, my head was down and tremendous sadness was written all over my face. Everyone kept telling me to smile, but none of them had any clue as to how sad I really was. When it came time for them to say "I do," I stood before the church all dressed in my flower girl attire and violently shook my head "No!" Oddly enough, I don't know if anyone ever even noticed my silent cry for help. It was a moment of marital bliss for them, and a moment of tremendous sorrow for me.

Years passed and the abuse became a normal part of my everyday life. I suffered in silence, yet I was greatly afraid of ever being found out as if it was me who was doing something wrong. My body seemed to betray me as the sensations I felt while he was molesting me were pleasurable. I believe this is what really cemented the feeling of guilt for me. How could my body enjoy something that felt so wrong?

My moment of deliverance came one day at school when we learned about sexual abuse. I remember being told that if anything had happened to me, I should tell my parent or another adult. This is when I gained the courage to tell Mom; another very vivid moment in time that I remember well.

By this time we no longer lived in that studio apartment. Mom had worked hard and had a new house built for us in the countryside. It was a two level wooden home with four bedrooms, two bathrooms, a living room, dining room, and nice sized kitchen. The floors were covered with a plush blush-colored carpet throughout the house and furnished very nicely. We had an elegant elongated wood dining table with six chairs where Mom often entertained company after church for dinner. On this day though, we would sit at the table to have a talk much different from any other we had had up to that point.

I had rehearsed over and over again what I would say to her that Friday afternoon just as I had learned at school. Mom sat and listened as I talked, never showing a bit of emotion. I told her how Sonny had been touching me, and that the people at school said I should tell if I was being abused. Mom assured me that she would speak with Sonny to find out from him what was going on, and she would let me know how it went after I returned home from my weekend stay with my cousin.

The weekend passed, and all I could focus on was wondering how it went...was he still there? Was he upset with me for telling? What would happen now? My cousin drove me home and I remember walking straight into the house and sitting at that same table to find out from Mom what happened.

These words I will never forget: "I talked to him. He said he didn't do it and that his ex-wife's daughter accused him of the same thing, but he didn't do it to either of you." My heart was crushed. Mom believed him over me, and on that very same night, I was molested once again by Sonny in her bed.

It is hard for me to accept that Mom knew nothing of what was happening to me, but I have forgiven her for not protecting me and for not believing me. The abuse continued, and I found other people to tell, but swore them all to secrecy. One little girl I had just met was the one person who spoke up for me and changed my life forever. She went against her vow of secrecy and told her mom. Her mom called my aunt, and the rest was history.

Sonny was eventually arrested when I was nine years old. We went to court, and I had to testify in front of him, his family, and a courtroom full of people about all the details of the abuse. Describing how he touched me and giving intricate details of what his penis looked like in front of strangers felt humiliating and so shameful. It was one of the most terrifying memories I have to date. I was afraid of him, what his family would say or do, and I was so concerned with speaking the whole truth and trying not to mess up any of the details.

Sonny was found guilty and sentenced to one year and one day. It seemed very unfair that he only had to spend a fraction of the time in prison for what he did to me for years, but soon I would learn that God is a God of justice. Sonny actually was released from prison early for good behavior, but he eventually paid the ultimate price for what he had done to me and many other girls. When he was released, he went blind, was bound to a wheelchair, and later died. I don't believe he was ever able to hurt another young girl, and that brings me great joy.

Unfortunately, the cycle of abuse did not end for me with Sonny. I was molested and raped by other members of his family, as well as my own family. This included males and females. The effect it had on my mentality was far greater than anything that happened to me physically. I grew up wondering *what is wrong with me, do I have a label on my forehead that says 'abuse me,' does this make me gay, people won't like me if they know the truth about me*, and on and on the negative thoughts went.

I believed I was not worthy of love because of all I had been through, yet I longed for love and attention *especially* from men. My father was present in my life, but he struggled with showing affection and I grew to resent him as time went on.

Sex became a way for me to numb the hurt I felt, and led me on a path of promiscuity and self-destruction. By the age of 15 I was pregnant with my first child, and gave birth to him when I was 16. The odds were stacked against me, and the victim role became my mentality.

Chapter 2 - God Still Had a Plan

As I look back on my life, I realize that every time I thought I was being rejected from something good, I was actually being redirected to something better.

--DR. STEVE MARABOLI

If you have never experienced abuse in any form, God bless you! For those of us who have, the experience impacts our lives in ways unimaginable. Sexual abuse robbed me of my childhood and innocence. Negative thinking ran rampant in my brain which ultimately shaped my life and experiences.

After being abused, my mindset was greatly impacted. Childhood dreams of growing up to be anything I wanted and believed I could be were stolen from me and replaced with feelings of being less than and unworthy of love. No longer was I free, but I felt bound to a life of being a victim. I believed and behaved as though I had no self-worth. Real love didn't seem possible for me, but really I didn't know how to love myself. How can you experience something you can't relate to or know nothing about?

During the process of going to court for what Sonny had done to me, I was connected to a counselor and underwent treatment to help with my recovery. As I was so young and really didn't know how to make sense of everything that happened, I honestly did not see a major benefit from counseling. Yes, it felt good to speak with someone and know that they believed me and did not judge me. However, the process I needed to learn was how to live the rest of my life without shame, guilt, bitterness, anger, or resentment. Those things were never taught to me, and so the torment continued.

After the initial experience with abuse, I never felt pretty and being ashamed of my body was something I actually picked up in elementary school. I'm sure it didn't help that I was often teased by friends and family about my body, or how often I was compared to my older sisters. Hurtful comments such as, "You look like the malnourished children in Africa" still sting and pierce my heart today as I remember how ugly that made me feel.

As a young child, I was all legs and arms with a short torso and big belly. All I remember hearing in reference to my looks were negative. On the other hand, my older sisters were always praised for their beauty and shapely physiques. In my mind, I was the ugly duckling of the family, inside and out.

In the fourth grade, I can recall wanting to finally do something to "fix" my body. So I developed a diet and exercise plan, and convinced my friend that she should do it with me. I guess you could say this is when my passion for helping others with fitness and nutrition was born. From that point on, my body was always something that needed fixing because I never felt good enough or that my body didn't measure up to what others thought was beautiful.

During my middle school years, I found that being sexually engaged allowed me a temporary escape from all the negative feelings I associated with my body, and so sex became like a drug for me. In addition to feeling inadequate, I became consumed with the idea of proving to myself that I was not gay during those years. At that point in my life I had been molested by four different females and I really believed something was wrong with me. It was such a shameful thing for me that I never found the courage to speak on it until I was an adult. In my young, tainted adolescent mind, the only way to prove to myself that I was not homosexual was to have sex with boys. This began in the seventh grade but as you can guess, I never found the peace I was looking for in those encounters. In fact, it did nothing but add to the guilt, shame, and feelings of inadequacy I already carried.

I didn't realize the damage I was doing to my spirit each time I offered my body in exchange for a few moments of pleasure. Guilt isolated me and I felt so alone. There was no way I could speak with my father or mother about the things I was feeling and doing. Daddy never hit me, but in my heart I knew he would have likely killed me if he had known. He was the strictest of strict, and played no games when it came to discipline. Mom was the other extreme, but at this time of my life, she was living overseas with her third husband and we didn't have the personal connection for me to feel comfortable with sharing any of what I was going through. Besides, I had tried living with her and her new husband in the United Kingdom, but he was very jealous of my relationship with Mom and ultimately made me feel unwanted there. So I spent my middle school years moving back and forth between Daddy's home in Huntsville and Mom's home in the United Kingdom, until Mom finally relocated to Marietta, Georgia in 1993.

The move to Georgia was tough on me emotionally. I had caused so much turmoil in my Dad's home during my Freshman year of high school that I had basically worn out my welcome, and now all I was left with was living with Mom and a man I knew hated me in a city where I had no friends.

We moved to Marietta in July; by November I was pregnant, and before I gave birth, Mom was divorced. Daddy stopped speaking to me for a long time as he was tremendously disappointed, but Mom was right by my side the entire time. She knew the experience of being a teen mom because it happened to her when she was 17. It also was not her first experience with having a teen daughter get pregnant as my oldest sister had also traveled this path.

There was no way for me to know how much my life would change with this new responsibility. My sisters begged me to abort the baby, but in my mind this was an answer to my prayers. God was giving me a child who would love me forevermore, and there was no way I was going to give up this great opportunity.

On July 23, 1994 at the age of 16, I almost lost my life in labor and delivery. The hospital room was like a circus with all of the chaos and commotion we had going on, but it was also beautiful. It had a homelike feel with beautiful hardwood floors, cozy dark cherry wood furniture, and enough space for all of the crew I had by my side. Mom, my sister, my best friend, and my cousin were there for the 18+ hours I was in labor. The doctor had given me too much anesthesia in my epidural, which caused me to turn extremely pale and caused uncontrollable shivers. The funniest moment, which was not funny at all at the time, was when I had accepted that I was going to die and bid farewell to everyone present in the room. My farewell speech made Mom a nervous wreck and she lost her mind with my nurse and made her cry. That was one of the first times I ever felt truly loved and protected by Mom. Throughout the whole ordeal, she never once left me alone.

After pushing for over three hours, my beautiful son Jordan was born. He was instantly the love of my life, the one I would always protect, and the one who would always love me in return. Immediately after Jordan's birth I began to hemorrhage and lost so much blood that the hospital staff could not believe I was still alive. The nurse told me she had never seen anyone alive with a blood count as low as mine. That was God. In spite of all my mistakes, He still had a plan and purpose for my life, but the road ahead would still be filled with ups and downs along with an abundance of uncertainty.

Chapter 3 - Destination Education

It is good to have an end to journey toward; but it is the journey that matters, in the end.

--ERNEST HEMINGWAY

Being pregnant in the tenth grade was a challenge in and of itself. Every day I was sick and unable to be in school. I ended up being in a special program where I stayed home and completed my schoolwork. A teacher from the school would come by my home each week to deliver my assignments and administer any tests I needed to take. Thankfully, I didn't fall behind and was able to return to school after giving birth to Jordan just before the start of my junior year.

Mom continued doing what she does best, working and providing. I must say that she was a great provider for Jordan and me, even though I did not show appreciation well. In my heart I felt as though Mom owed me something for the abuse I experienced, and I still harbored a lot of anger, bitterness, and resentment towards her. My heart longed for her affection and attention, but she didn't have that to give.

There were many times that finances were a struggle for us, but things always worked out. We moved around a lot when Jordan was a baby, and I ended up attending three different high schools by the time I was a senior. My senior year is when things began to fall apart for me as I lost focus on the importance of education.

I wanted to make money to help with caring for Jordan, so I took a part-time job at a couple of fast-food restaurants. It wasn't long before I realized that was not the life for me. Being in school all day, working all evening, and staying up with my baby all night was not giving me what I thought I needed. I ended up missing over 100 days of school during my senior year, and I wanted so badly to just drop out.

Mom was very busy with work and always out of town for her job, which often left me home alone to manage with Jordan. Soon, partying and hanging with my friends took priority over school and working. Even though I was not of age, somehow I was in the club practically every weekend with my best friend. We both loved to dance and the attention we drew from men, so this became our life.

Clubbing turned into drinking alcohol frequently and eventually trying marijuana. My life was going nowhere fast. I put Jordan and myself in several dangerous situations just by being reckless with my life. It is only by the grace of God that neither of us was ever physically harmed, or that I didn't find myself in jail. God was still showing that He had a plan and a purpose for me.

After missing so many days of school with no explanation, the truancy officer from my high school showed up at our house. It was no secret that I had been missing school, so Mom was not surprised by the visit. I had been making a case with her for me to go to an alternative school for pregnant and teen moms where I could earn my high school diploma in my own time. By missing so many days, I was failing all of my classes. When I was present, I slept through every single class. You can imagine just how much my teachers loved me!

Mom scheduled a meeting with my school counselor right away. I don't remember that counselor's name, but I'm eternally grateful to her and Mom for what they did for me that day we met. They both begged me not to drop out and to get rid of the idea of going to an alternative school. My counselor asked that if she was able to get all of my teachers to agree to let me make-up all of my missed assignments, would I be willing to do the work so I could graduate. My answer was yes even though I was still very skeptical of how it would all work out.

It wasn't until one of my teachers made a spiteful comment to me that I found determination to prove what I was capable of. I don't remember her name or what she looked like, but I clearly remember her saying to me, "You will never graduate! There is no way possible that you will make up all of these missed assignments before graduation." At that very moment, a fire was lit in my belly and I vowed that I would do everything in my power to finish school on time. And that's exactly what I did.

Needless to say, I didn't finish with high grades. I actually finished by the skin of my teeth with all 70s in my classes (in Georgia, anything below 70 is failing). In fact, the week of graduation I still had a 60 in one of my classes and had to do extra work to bring it up before I could graduate. Even though it was very difficult, I will never forget that sense of pride that came over me when I saw my final grades and knew that I would be able to walk across that stage with my class.

Graduation day was one of the best days of my life. There wasn't a lot of my family present for that day, but those who were will always hold a special place in my heart. I was shot down by some of my closest relatives when I invited them to my graduation. They basically told me it wasn't worth them coming because it wasn't like I graduated with honors. Another wound was added to my heart, but I still beamed with pride for that entire day.

With high school behind me, it was time to plan out my next chapter in life. I was ready to gain my independence and move away from Mom for college; well, not exactly, but that is how it worked out. Mom promised to pay for a place for me to live as long as I stayed in school, and so she helped me to re-locate back to Huntsville.

Jordan and I were now on our own. My first place was nothing lavish, but it was ours. It had two bedrooms, one and a half bathrooms, a spacious living room with a dining area, and a small kitchen. Mom allowed me to bring furniture from home, so it had a "home" feeling about it. The worst aspects about it were the horrible puke-colored shag carpet, the refrigerator with no separate freezer, and the area where it was located. Still, I was grateful to finally be on my own and back in Huntsville.

For the first several weeks, we had no food, home phone, or car for transportation. We sat in the apartment alone together while I hoped and prayed for anyone to show up. There was never a microwave or cable, so I learned to cook daily and the local television stations became our best friends.

It was less than two months before Mom surprised me with a car. My friends teased me about how small it was, but it didn't stop them from riding in it. Soon my place became the hangout for all of my friends, and I was back into my old ways.

When it came time for my first year of college to begin, I did not take it seriously. I registered and dropped out after three days on campus. Mom kept true to her word and refused to help me pay for my apartment, so I had to find a job to support Jordan and keep a roof over our heads.

I worked in retail for several months and wanted to enlist in the military. When that didn't work out, I took a full-time job in a local manufacturing plant. It was in that plant where I realized that education was my ticket out of poverty and so I enrolled myself in a local university and began my college career almost two years after graduating high school.

Chapter 4 - Independence Comes with a Price

The best way out is always through.

--ROBERT FROST

Being on my own wasn't as easy as I had hoped, but I loved my independence. Even though Mom began helping me with my rent again when I went back to school, working the various jobs I had prior to enrolling full-time as a college student taught me responsibility and what it felt like to be able to provide for my son.

Jordan was growing fast; actually, we were growing up together. He was the best child a parent could ask for. He never gave me any trouble and basically kept himself entertained.

Shortly after I began school, so did Jordan. At the age of four, I enrolled him in the Head Start Program which serves children of low income families. Because I was so young, I had no idea of the importance of early childhood education. Consequently, Jordan was behind the other kids. The teacher had problems getting him to stay in his seat and to pay attention for any length of time. It wasn't until one special teacher grew attached to Jordan and poured time into him that he was able to catch up and do well in school.

By my second semester of school, I landed an on-campus job where I worked for 20 hours per week in between classes and caring for Jordan. College was tough, but I was doing much better than I did my last year of high school. My personal life was still a mess, but I was able to keep going.

I kept searching for love from a man, but never quite found it. When love did present itself, I didn't know how to appreciate it because I was so accustomed to being mistreated or rejected. If the guy wasn't abusing me physically, or raping me, it didn't feel like love to me. Again, abuse had become my normal.

I dated many drug dealers and other guys who had absolutely nothing going for themselves. At some point, I stopped expecting to be in a relationship and was just content with being in a man's presence. In some respect, my heart grew cold and I lost all desire for affection. Through my life's experiences I learned to suppress my feelings and not deal with my emotions, so that seemed to help me cope for a long time. Perhaps this was to protect my heart from further damage or disappointment, but it worked well for the guys I dated because I came with no strings attached.

After moving back to Huntsville, Daddy and I got back on good terms. I remember how proud he was when I got back into school; I loved making him proud. He loved Jordan, and Jordan loved him. My father had five daughters, and no sons; I was his youngest child. Jordan was his second grandson, but the only grandson who lived nearby. We would visit him often and took great pleasure in going to his house to watch boxing. It was one of our favorite sports to watch, and it was always more fun watching it with Daddy. Whenever his favorite boxer was winning, he would be so full of life and excitement. His laugh was contagious, and everything felt right in those moments.

My father battled type 2 diabetes for years. The disease caused him to have his leg amputated when I was a little girl, and he was forced into retirement when I moved back to Huntsville because of his failing health. He was on dialysis for several years, but by this time, things were not looking so good.

Just before Thanksgiving 1999, my father had to go into the hospital for an infection he developed in his foot. The doctors were going to try to save his foot by doing a procedure to increase blood flow to the area. He made it through the procedure, but never healed from it. He was in an incredible amount of pain, and the meds often had him out of his right mind. I spent many nights sleeping by his bedside, or in the waiting room with my stepmom and sisters.

Two months after my father was admitted, I received an urgent phone call from my aunt to get to the hospital right away. I was instructed not to drive, but no one would tell me what was going on. On the ride there with my cousin, I kept hoping for the best. We listed every possible outcome, but I knew in my heart that he was gone. As I braced myself to enter his hospital room, my fears were confirmed when I saw him lying peacefully in that bed. Family members were gathered around and weeping at his bedside.

My heart was filled with great sorrow. I was broken. The reality of that moment hit me fast and hard. I would never hear his laugh again, or hear him proudly refer to me as "Daddy's Joy Joy." Thoughts were racing through my mind. How could this be? Things were just getting good between us, and now he's dead. I hadn't done enough to make him proud. I wanted him to see me graduate. I wanted more talks with him. I wanted him to be a big part of Jordan's life - the consistent positive male figure he so desperately needed but didn't have. I wished I hadn't wasted so many years being mad at my Dad, but none of my wishes and wants mattered anymore. Daddy was gone and there was nothing I could do about it.

The first two years of college were rough. I lost three very important people in my life: my grandmother, my aunt, and then my father. My grades suffered as I fell back into old habits of not showing up for classes. Before long, I was on academic probation and pleading my case before an advisor to not kick me out of school.

Tragedy seemed to be on the rise after the death of my father. Mom's business was on the decline and she wasn't able to support herself or me any longer. Quitting school was not an option because, even though he was no longer living, I had to do something to make Daddy proud. Initially I began working two jobs while going to school full-time to support Jordan and me, but things started getting way too hectic. We were eating pizza literally every day - so much that one worker at Domino's remembered my name and address when I ran into them at their new job. Jordan's grades began to decline because I didn't have the time to help him with his schoolwork. Honestly, I didn't have much time for Jordan, period. I was always running and extremely stressed out.

Although I had to rely on food stamps and other government assistance previously, I never saw myself having to live in low income housing. I had too much pride for that, yet here I was faced with a decision of whether to continue struggling to survive while going to school, or let go of my pride and move into a low income apartment. I chose the latter, and thank God I did.

From the moment I moved into that apartment, I had a plan. I was going to finish school, get a good paying job, and buy a home for Jordan and me. However, things got more complicated before they got easier.

One year after my move, I was pregnant once again. The father of my unborn child and I were already not on good terms, and I had no idea of how I would support another child on my own with the little amount of money I was earning from my part-time job. I went into a deep depression, and Jordan, who was now nearly eight years old, was left to fend for himself. Most days I couldn't pull myself out of bed long enough to do anything. Jordan became responsible for getting himself ready for school, as I lay in bed drowning in my sorrows. I began missing classes again, but this time I was smart enough to withdraw.

The pregnancy came with many challenges. I went into pre-term labor during my sixth month of pregnancy and had to go on bed rest. Being on bed rest meant I couldn't work and earn an income. This thought alone threw me into a deeper depression, but God still took care of us.

My daughter Jaden was born on October 13, 2002. Her delivery was much easier than what I experienced with Jordan. I was in labor for less than six hours with no epidural. With three pushes, she was out and already talking! Jaden was perfect and beautiful from the moment she entered this world, and once again, when I laid eyes on her, it was love at first sight.

One week after giving birth to Jaden, I developed a persistent headache that would not go away no matter what medicine I took. At first I thought that I may have been doing too much. Coming home with Jaden was very different to when I came home with Jordan. I was on my own this time and had to do everything for myself with no help. So naturally, I thought rest was all I needed to feel better.

The kids and I spent my first weekend out of the hospital with my cousin, Von. She was in love with both of my children and took care of them like they were her own; much like she did for me when I was a little girl before Sonny ever came into the picture. Von was like a second mother to me and was a great help. That weekend Von allowed me to relax while she cared for Jaden, but nothing I did helped my headache whatsoever.

By the time I arrived at home that Sunday evening, my head felt like it was about to explode. I called Mom at 3 AM in tears and begged her to come over to check my blood pressure. Blood pressure had never been an issue for me, but at that moment, God placed it in my spirit that I needed to have it checked.

Mom came right away, and sure enough, my blood pressure was extremely high. She immediately took me to the emergency room. All I could do was cry because I was so afraid I was about to die and leave my two children motherless. Mom kept trying to reassure me that I would be fine, and telling me to relax so my blood pressure wouldn't go up any higher.

The emergency room staff got me into a dark room right away to keep from further agitating my enormous migraine. When I was asked to provide a urine sample, I did not recognize myself as I saw my reflection in the mirror when entering the restroom. My face was swollen so badly that I no longer looked human. To make matters worse, the doctors and nurses had no clue what was wrong with me and kept predicting the worst possible outcomes. At first they said it was congestive heart failure, and then it was an aneurism. It wasn't until my OB-GYN came that we found out I had atypical toxemia. In normal cases, toxemia is developed during pregnancy and the cure is to induce labor. However, in my case, the baby was already born and the toxemia came afterwards.

I was admitted into the hospital, and before getting settled in my room, I had a seizure while holding Jaden in my arms and nursing her. When I regained consciousness, I was surrounded by all of my family members whose eyes were filled with tears. I had no recollection of anything that happened. According to what I was told by my family, when questioned by my doctors, I didn't know my age, who the president was, or any other facts I would ordinarily know. Hence the reason for all of their tears.

My doctor kept me in the hospital for nearly a week, and I was once again confined to the bed on doctor's orders. Jaden was not able to stay with me because the doctor was afraid that too much stimulation would cause me to have another seizure. Those days in that hospital bed were the loneliest times of my life. I cried many tears as I longed to be with my newborn baby and Jordan, but couldn't. Once more, God spared my life.

I didn't know how I was going to make it, but I was now more determined than ever to accomplish my goals. Jordan and Jaden deserved it, and God kept showing me that there was a profound purpose for me to still be here.

Chapter 5 - Dreams Do Come True

*To accomplish great things, we must not only act, but also
dream; not only plan, but also believe.*

--ANATOLE FRANCE

So there I was at the age of 25 with two children,
raising them alone, and trying to figure out life. College
was on the backburner for a few months after Jaden was
born, and I wasn't sure how I would manage to care for her
and Jordan, go to school, and work. Before I could really
wrap my brain around it and get bogged down in stress, a
miraculous opportunity was presented to me.

Von and her husband stepped in and saved our lives.
They had both grown extremely attached to Jaden while
she stayed with them during my time in the hospital.
Without ever having to ask for a thing, they gave me
money at random times, just because, bought more clothes
than Jaden could ever use, and became a constant presence
in our lives. When my car was repossessed, they gave me
one of theirs. When I needed a job, they helped me start my
own corporation so I could work from home and be there
with Jaden. When I needed someone to watch the kids
while I went to class, Von volunteered. When they found
out how much debt I was in, they helped me pay it off.
Everything I could ever need, they helped me to achieve it.

I will never forget the day they told me exactly why they were so eager to help. Years before they became successful, they too struggled and faced a lot of debt. Not many people knew, but somehow my father did. He stepped in and helped them when no one else did, and now they had the ability to pay it forward to his child.

Because of their love and support, I was able to attend classes year round. When Von wasn't able to keep Jaden during the day, God sent another angel who kept her free of charge simply because she wanted to see me graduate. I made the Dean's list for several semesters, and I graduated in less than two years of Jaden being born.

A few months before beginning my final semester of school, I was able to move my little family into a brand new, never-lived-in three bedroom apartment. It was the most beautiful apartment in the world in my eyes, and came complete with vaulted ceilings, two full bathrooms, a nice sized kitchen, a full laundry room, and a balcony. It was a far cry from the stuffy old two bedroom Section 8 apartment we lived in for three years prior to that.

Things were looking up and my dreams were becoming reality. The local newspaper even featured my story in an article highlighting my achievements as a single mother when I graduated. College graduation was much different from high school graduation. I had a huge outpouring of support from family and friends near and far. That day was one of the happiest days of my life and we celebrated it to the fullest. My family threw a huge cookout for everyone who came. It was the true definition of eating, drinking, and being merry!

Soon after graduation, one of my closest friends got married and I was bitten by the love bug. I wanted a relationship that resulted in my husband looking at me the way her husband looked at her as she walked down the aisle. The same weekend of her wedding, I met a guy. We seemed to hit it off right away, and spent the entire evening talking until the sun was almost up the next morning. Naively, I allowed him to come to my apartment to continue our conversation. That same night, I was raped by him; only this time I didn't want to call it rape so I made him my instant boyfriend.

Before long, my new rapist boyfriend was living with me. He was an alcoholic with no car and had no job, but I wanted so badly to love him. I was tired of being hurt, tired of being in and out of relationships. This one had to work and I was determined to make it happen.

While I continued to pretend we were in love and went so far as to begin shopping for wedding rings, things got progressively worse. He stole from me and we often fought in front of my kids, but every Sunday, we were at church together like all was well with our souls. His parents adored my children and me, yet they had no clue of the torment I faced when I was alone with their son. Jordan was afraid of him, and I, for whatever reason, just kept holding on. The rape continued and I became completely repulsed by sex. For the first time in my adult life, I didn't want to be touched.

I began neglecting my business and was forced to begin looking for a job outside of the home. The first company I interviewed with hired me for a position that paid higher than anything I had ever made. It was a temp-to-hire position with a prominent company in my area and I would be doing work relative to my field of study. God was still blessing me.

A couple of weeks into my new job, my boyfriend raped me once again. This time he got me pregnant. I was devastated. Life was just turning around for me and I knew that neither of us could afford another child. While I was depressed, he was elated. I called my Mom and sister in hysterical tears. What was I to do now? Mom assured me that I didn't have to worry, God had my back. Even though I didn't have a clue what she meant, I trusted what Mom told me. Before I had a chance to experience morning sickness, I miscarried. When the nurse at the hospital delivered the news to confirm the miscarriage, she looked quite puzzled as there was no hint of sadness on my face. I wanted to turn cartwheels in that room! God heard my cry and gave me another chance.

Time went on and I eventually kicked my boyfriend out of my apartment. I retrieved my key from him, but later learned that he stole it back without me knowing. One night I heard him outside my apartment talking to his friend. He was drunk and talking loud about what he was going to do to me because he thought I wasn't home. I lay in my bed listening to the whole thing, but not afraid at all because I just knew he couldn't get in. The kids were gone so I was home alone. I listened as he walked up the stairs to my door and told his friend good-bye. Imagine my surprise when I heard him put the key in the lock and open the door. My heart dropped to my ankles. He entered my bedroom and was startled to see me there. His plan, as he explained to me, was to sit in my bedroom in the dark to wait for me to get home so he could kill me. In all the time we had been together, he had never hit me. So I didn't take his threats that night seriously; however, he did hit me and took my phone from me so I could not call the police.

The next morning I was able to escape the apartment while he was passed out on my sofa. I called his sister and she sent their father to get him out of my apartment. His father begged me not to call the police and assured me that his son would never do anything like that again. Even after all of that, I didn't cut ties with him completely.

I felt like damaged goods and didn't believe that anyone could love me. I believed I was unworthy of love. One of my family members even asked me why was it so hard for me to keep a man. In my defense, I told her that none of them had been worth keeping. Honestly speaking, that was never really a thought in my mind, but now I wondered if it should be. Why was it so hard for me to keep a man?

In spite of my failed relationships, I continued to do well in my job. I was hired full-time as a permanent employee and received a $20,000 raise. You couldn't tell me I wasn't rich! Immediately I was obsessed with finding a house to complete the dream I envisioned when I first moved into those low income apartments.

Within a year of starting my new job, I purchased

my brand new, custom built, full brick home. It was perfect for us; four bedrooms, two baths, a big living room, eat-in kitchen, fenced in backyard, and two car garage. My favorite part was the Jacuzzi tub in the master bathroom along with the huge walk-in closet. It was my dream come true, and to top it off, it was located in an awesome school district for the kids. The neighborhood was quiet and many of my neighbors were police officers. Jordan was in the sixth grade and Jaden had just turned three years old. Finally, I felt accomplished and I did it all without the help of a man or anyone else. We moved into our new home on my 28th birthday - what a great birthday that was!

Eventually, I cut ties with my ex and moved on to the next abusive relationship, which lasted for a year. After this failed relationship attempt, I was convinced that I was wearing a stamp across my forehead that read "Abuse Me!" Clearly something I was doing was attracting the same type of people into my life. My first time watching "The Secret" opened my eyes to many things, including how my thoughts were attracting these negative experiences into my life over and over again. It was time for a change.

With all of my goals achieved, I had nothing else to work towards and I felt lost. Relationships were clearly not my thing, so I decided I would focus on finding out what made me happy. I took a vow of celibacy and went on my first trip without my children or family. It was a girls' trip to New Orleans for a big music festival I had never heard of, but I was excited to take on this new adventure. It was finally time to focus on making Joy happy, and I was loving every second of this fresh start.

Chapter 6 - On the Brink

Success is the ability to go from failure to failure without losing your enthusiasm.

--WINSTON CHURCHILL

A whole month after our girls' trip to New Orleans, I met a new guy online. I was skeptical about meeting him in person and wanted my friends to check him out first on my behalf. They were both married, so I trusted their judgment way more than I trusted my own.

He lived in another state, but not too far away. We spent hours on the phone getting to know each other for a few weeks before we finally decided to meet in person. My friends never got the chance to check him out until well after we were already an item. Our first date was a bit awkward, but it ended with a kiss that swept me off my feet.

We began taking turns traveling to visit each other, celibacy went out the window and before long, I was pregnant. Jordan was 13 at the time and Jaden had just celebrated her 5th birthday. This time it felt different. He wasn't freaking out, but I was. He had one child already and was established with his own place and job. I was afraid of being alone with three children to raise on my own, so I immediately began talking about marriage. I was emailing him pictures of rings I wanted practically every day, and questioning when he was going to make the move to Alabama.

I turned 30 years old during this pregnancy, and this one came with even more complications. I was diagnosed with gestational diabetes and hospitalized for a few days for monitoring as I learned to inject my pregnant belly with insulin and prick my finger to check my blood sugar. I was a nervous, paranoid wreck as all of this reminded me of the many years I watched Daddy battle diabetes and how his life ended. My boyfriend was there with me through it all. It was the first time I experienced having a positive relationship with my child's father while pregnant, and the first time I had been with a guy who could support me financially. As my pregnant belly grew bigger, he and I grew closer.

Our son Landen was born on June 3rd, 2008 with both of us present to see him enter the world. Mom, Jordan, Jaden, my sister, and godmother were there to greet our new child as well. When Landen was delivered, the cord was wrapped around his neck and his face was blue. My heart stood still until I heard the sound of his cry. Holding my newborn baby in my arms while surrounded by all the people I knew loved me made my life feel complete. Here I was with yet another beautiful blessing from God.

We left the hospital together as a family, and my soon-to-be fiancé stayed to take care of us for three weeks. Symptoms of toxemia began to resurface during my first week at home, but this time I knew the signs and called my doctor right away. I had to begin taking blood pressure medication immediately to avoid hospitalization; unfortunately, the high blood pressure did not go away this time around and I was at high risk of getting type 2 diabetes like my father.

Jaden and Jordan both grew attached to my fiancé, but Jaden followed him everywhere he went. One evening while grilling outside together, she asked him if she could call him "Papi." He was honored, and they grew even closer. It delighted me to see that he loved my children, and they loved him. He knew my past, and yet he still loved me. He even encouraged me to get group counseling for my sisters, Mom, and me. We did as he suggested, and it was the beginning of our healing as a family.

A few days before Landen's first birthday, we were married and feeling on top of the world. My husband had relocated to Alabama and took a job with significantly less pay. Finances would be tight, but at least we would be together and our child would have both parents in the home.

Four months after we said "I do," I was laid off from my job of five years. I was convinced that God had a sense of humor, but I was also extremely grateful that I did not have to go through that hardship alone. My husband and I were members of a local church that we attended faithfully, and we were both working hard to strengthen our connection with God. While I was laid off, I spent a lot of time getting to know God through reading His Word and watching Christian television programs. I found strength and comfort in listening to teachings by Joyce Meyer and Joel Osteen. They became my spiritual mentors, especially Joyce. Joyce had experienced sexual abuse like I had, and her realness just drew me in. I had tried having a relationship with God many times before, but guilt and shame always kept me away from receiving His love.

With nothing but time on my hands, I devoted myself to learning about God and seeking His purpose for my life. Before being laid off, I knew that my purpose was not being fulfilled in that job; however, I was comfortable there and was afraid of getting out of my comfort zone. In my heart, I knew that I was supposed to be doing something to help women and using my testimony to help with the healing of others. It had always been a dream of mine since I was a young child to become a hair stylist, but that dream was always looked down upon by Mom who seemed highly embarrassed anytime someone asked what I wanted to be when I grew up and my response was "a cosmetologist." I saw this lay off as a blessing and a way to reconnect with what I wanted to do as a child, and a means of connecting with women. So I began researching local beauty schools and the requirements for obtaining my license. My husband was not thrilled by the idea at all, no matter how much I fasted and prayed for God to change his mind. It didn't seem fair, but I was no longer independent Joy; I was now someone's wife.

When I received an offer to return to my former place of employment as a federal employee instead of a contractor as I was before, my husband was convinced that

I should take the job. *He* was convinced, but I wasn't. In fact, I was actually depressed over the situation as it was no longer a decision I could make on my own. Being a submissive wife wasn't something I was good at, but it was something I was desperately working hard to learn how to become. I sought counsel from my bishop, I prayed with my friends, I cried before God, and in the end, I reluctantly took the job. All aspirations of being a successful entrepreneur helping other women went out of the window.

I returned to work three months after being laid off on December 21st. Instead of being home with my family to bring in the holiday, I was at work on Christmas Eve because I had no paid time off. Christmas has always been my favorite time of year, and I have always gone above and beyond for my kids each year from the time Jordan and I were on our own. Christmas 2009 was the first time I had ever experienced having nothing to give my children and I felt like a failure. I knew that "Jesus was the reason for the season," but I still longed to see my children filled with excitement and joy when they woke up Christmas morning. That day at work, a co-worker randomly came in and began handing out $100 bills to those of us there. In that moment, I knew God was once again showing me that He hears our cries and I was overtaken with gratitude. Because of one man's generosity, I was able to buy a gift for each member of my family that year.

God continued to show me favor, and things began to turn around for our family. Jordan and I had become very involved in the drama ministry at our church. Acting was a passion we both had in common. While I was discovering that I enjoyed public speaking, Jordan found a love for writing plays. We attended Bible Study together as a family most Wednesday nights, and each Sunday morning, we were seated in the front of the church together. My family had come a long way, but tragedy was not far off.

Abuse still played a significant role in my daily life without me even realizing it. Intimacy became an issue in my marriage and my husband and I began to slowly drift apart. I felt rejected by him and he felt emotionally disconnected from me. We spent many days and nights being isolated from one another; him in his man cave, and me in my bedroom. I was in graduate school working on my MBA in addition to working my full-time job and taking care of our family. Our work schedules were in conflict with each other, so we typically only saw each other in passing. I began resenting my husband and feeling like a married single parent.

Communication was not one of our strong points. Little spats turned into weeks of not speaking to each other. The home atmosphere was often tense, and I felt extremely lonely once again. We argued a lot about money and things escalated when he lost his mother unexpectedly. He felt unsupported by me, and I felt unloved by him.

Shortly thereafter, I discovered that he had been communicating frequently with a young lady he worked with. When I confronted him about it, we had a huge fight which resulted in him leaving home. My world came crashing down. I sought guidance from my bishop and within a couple of days my husband returned home. We went on as if nothing happened, and I didn't question him again about the other lady.

At the same time, Jordan had been going through a rebellious stage during his senior year of high school. He began showing up at home drunk and we suspected he was smoking pot. Things got tense and Jordan left home for several days. My husband and I continuously argued over Jordan not being ready to move away for college. I wanted to buy a car for Jordan and help him get in school, but my husband did not agree.

During her third grade year, Jaden began battling depression and speaking of wanting to harm herself. She told her schoolteacher that she wanted to kill herself because her dad was not in her life. Her father and I had not spoken since Jaden was a baby, and when I did attempt to reach out to him, it turned into a full out screaming match. My father had always been present in my life, so the pain my daughter was experiencing was not familiar to me. It didn't matter that my husband had been good to her. She watched him interact with Landen and longed for that same type of relationship with her biological father. Making matters worse for her, Jordan connected with his biological father just before I got married and often traveled to Georgia to visit with his dad's family. Jaden felt alone and unloved, and I didn't know how to fix it.

Three years into my marriage, life had become chaotic and my stress level was through the roof. I was working long hours and weekends for a special project at work when I began experiencing chest pains. My co-workers rushed me to the emergency room. Between school, work, my failing marriage, and dealing with the things my children were experiencing, I had forgotten to put taking care of me as one of my priorities. My weight had increased significantly and my blood pressure was hard to control. I was on several prescription medications and nothing was working. Thankfully, there was nothing wrong with my heart when I was examined at the hospital that day, but it served as a wake-up call.

Jordan's graduation that year was the turning point of my marriage. My husband and I had grown completely apart and it was most evident on that day. I was determined more than ever that I was going to go against what he told me and get Jordan enrolled in the university of his choosing. Rebellious Joy had been awakened, and nothing good can ever come from that!

Chapter 7 - God is Still Faithful

A winner is just a loser who tried one more time.

--GEORGE M. MOORE, JR.

The evil three (anger, bitterness, and resentment) were brewing in my spirit for a long time, and going unchecked. The emotions I didn't allow myself to deal with didn't magically go away; they were still there and causing strife in my life without me being aware. They played out in my marriage, relationships with family, on my job, and, more importantly, in the way I felt about myself.

Everything was falling apart around me, and now this evil brew in my spirit was in full control of me. In relationships, I typically struggled with being fully committed and faithful (if I wasn't fully committed, I could be less caring if they did something to screw me over); however, this had never been an issue with my husband. He had my full undivided attention - that is until I decided I wanted vengeance.

Although I never brought up that other woman again, the thought of her still lurked in the back of my mind. I knew the importance of forgiveness, yet I withheld it from my husband. All I could focus on was how unfair it was to me for him to pursue someone else after all I had done for him. The evil three has a tendency to make one very self-centered and solely focused on being victimized.

I decided that I deserved love, and would find it outside of my marriage. To my detriment, I reconnected with an ex who previously brought me nothing but pain. This time around, everything seemed so different. My mind blocked out the fact that he had physically abused me before, slept with multiple women while we dated, and never showed me any respect. At this point in my life, my twisted mind saw him as my loving savior - rescuing me from a pit of loneliness and despair. When my conscience would remind me that I was married, I would remind my conscience that my behavior was justified because my so-called "better half" did it first.

Three months into the affair, my conscience got the best of me and I confessed to my husband what I had done. He was in total shock and disbelief, which soon turned into rage. We had multiple screaming matches in front of the kids, and even came close to physical blows a couple of times. He told everyone he knew (including my two young children) that I had been sleeping around with other men.

I made the confession because I couldn't live with myself knowing that he didn't have a clue about what was going on. Although he and I had not been intimate in several months, I felt it was only fair to let him know so he could decide if he wanted to work things out or not. He decided it wasn't worth working out and moved away within a few weeks of my confession.

Even though I never expected him to stay, my heart

yearned for him to fight for me and not walk away so easily. It didn't seem fair that I dealt with his infidelity and never walked out, but I had already been taught that life wasn't fair. I felt abandoned, used, and overwhelmed, yet I would never allow him to see that. There I was once again on my own left to figure out the pieces of my life.

The divorce was finalized within seven months of my now ex-husband leaving. I was drowning in debt and many days I just wanted to run away from my life. Our bills we created together were left for me to handle on my own, and I had no support for taking care of the kids. On paper, I made great money, but in reality, I couldn't afford to feed my children and was one paycheck away from losing everything I owned. There was tremendous pressure for me to keep things together because my job security could be jeopardized if I could not manage my finances properly. I held things together the best I could while things continued to escalate.

Jordan was away at college and, unbeknownst to me, was having a difficult time coping with not being able to be home to support me through the divorce. Whenever he was home, we butted heads constantly. He had turned into a person I no longer recognized. I knew he was still drinking, but I never suspected that he actually had a problem. After all, I drank and smoked when I was young and remained in control.

In the midst of everything that was going on, I still had the responsibility of caring for Landen and Jaden. My baby boy was four at the time, and Jaden had just turned

10. The divorce was hard on the both of them. I would often find Landen sitting in his room in a daze with a look of total sadness all over his face. He was not accustomed to living without his dad and couldn't understand why he was no longer at home with us. Jaden didn't show her emotions much; she was more fixated on watching me to see how I was feeling.

I determined that I had to pick up the pieces and make life as normal as possible for my two little ones. With graduate school behind me, I had more time to invest in my children and do things that brought them happiness. Through watching Joyce Meyer, I learned the power of confessing God's Word out loud. I went through the Bible and wrote out faith confessions based on scripture and I began teaching them to Jaden and Landen. I watched my daughter turn into a more confident, self-loving little girl. She had always been extremely shy, especially around people she did not know. In fact, she would go completely mute if anyone she didn't know said anything to her. Speaking faith confessions seemed to help her believe in herself and changed her into being more outgoing. Jaden had always excelled academically and had been involved in the gifted program at her school since the third grade. With her newfound confidence, she was now ready to branch out into sports and eventually took it upon herself to find a basketball team to join.

I poured my heart into supporting Jaden in basketball, and learning ways to help Landen find peace with not seeing his father regularly. The kids were loving having my undivided attention and gradually the pain of my failed marriage had less of an impact on us all. Through sheer divine intervention, I was able to reconnect Jaden with her father. We spoke and made peace with our differences from the past, and they were reunited at last. It was a dream come true for my little girl that made a significant impact on her life.

That year, I had the opportunity to take the kids on vacation with Mom to Disney World in Orlando. Jordan was staying away at school for the summer to work on campus, so it was just the little ones and me living it up in Florida. It was Landen's first time there and we had a blast. Money was still extremely tight, but I saved just enough cash to allow us to have a great time with nothing left to spare when we returned home.

In spite of all that happened, things seemed to be going very well. Although Jordan and I still butted heads from time to time, he was doing a lot better and I could see a tremendous change in his behavior. His grades for the semester were not great at all, but I was so proud of him for landing his on-campus job. It appeared that sending him away to college wasn't a mistake after all; that is, until the morning of Landen's fifth birthday when everything in my world was turned upside down.

We had just made it back home from Orlando and I still had an extra day off from work to celebrate Landen's big day. Jordan had come home while we were out of town, which ended in us having a huge blow up before he returned to school that Sunday. That next morning while lying in bed, I received a phone call on my cell phone.

When I answered, the operator informed me that I had a collect call from a Tuscaloosa County inmate. Since I knew no inmates in Tuscaloosa County, I did not accept the call and went on with plans to celebrate my baby's special day. The calls kept coming in, and I kept rejecting each call until one of my co-workers convinced me that I should accept the next one. At this point, I began trying to contact Jordan. We had not spoken since he left the day before, but I was certain that this call could in no way be from my son.

Jordan's phone rang straight to voicemail and now I was in a panic. I contacted my cousin Jordan rode back to school with to see if he had seen him that morning; he had not. A few minutes later, my cousin called back to say, "Joy, I am so sorry. Jordan was arrested this morning as he walked to work on campus. I don't know why, but I believe it had something to do with drugs." I'm certain that my heart stopped beating as I listened on the phone in disbelief. *Arrested? Jordan? He has never even been so much as written up in school. This couldn't be possible. And for drugs?* There had to be some type of mistake.

Through all the years of raising my son, I never fathomed that he would ever be in trouble with the law. I had preached so much to him about safe sex, ensuring he didn't make a baby, but jail never even crossed my mind. Sure, I spoke with him about the consequences of his choices if he was smoking pot and got caught, but even still that seemed so farfetched to my brain. Yet here I was, sitting in my bathroom screaming, crying harder than ever before down the phone to my dear friend after confirming that my son had been arrested on two drug charges.

On that day, it felt as though my world ended. Nothing in life had prepared me for that moment. We were supposed to be celebrating Landen's fifth birthday, but instead, I was in mourning for my then 18-year-old son. With all of my money spent during our vacation, I didn't know how I would ever be able to afford to get Jordan out. Furthermore, I didn't even know where to begin in the process. My mind was stuck on how this ever happened, and how it happened to *my* child. He had never been in any trouble up to that point and now he was facing two felony charges with a bond of $30K per charge.

Jordan knew that the cops were after him because a few months prior to his arrest, they searched his dorm room for drugs. They didn't find anything there, but they promised him that they were on to him and would be back. With all that I had been going through with the divorce, he took it upon himself not to burden me with that information. Instead, he decided to work a few jobs so he could hire a lawyer to represent him.

With the help of my family, we were able to hire the attorney Jordan had been working with and get his bond lowered; the only problem was that my son had to stay locked up for nearly five days before we were able to get him released. Those were the hardest five days of my entire life and the whole experience trumped everything I had ever faced up to that point. I spent each day in tears with no ability to focus on anything other than knowing my son was behind bars. In my lowest moments, I turned to God for comfort. He was still there for me, waiting with open arms. He reminded me of His awesomeness when my sweet little

Landen broke out in song one morning as I was driving them to summer camp. The song on his lips was "My God is Awesome." It became my personal anthem throughout the whole ordeal.

I learned a lot about my first born in a short amount of time. What I thought was just a teenage thing he would grow out of turned out to be a real problem with alcoholism and addiction. Immediately after picking him up from jail that day, we carried him to treatment and he has been clean and sober ever since. It didn't feel good at all during that time, but what came out of it was a tremendous blessing from God. My son was saved from a life of addiction, and now he had a testimony that he didn't mind sharing with the world. When he was arrested, he was facing 40 years in prison, but in the end, one of the cases was dropped and he was sentenced to two years of probation. God had proven to me once again that He was still faithful and there was nothing too hard for Him.

Chapter 8 - Conquering Fear

Courage is resistance to fear, mastery of fear - not absence of fear.

--MARK TWAIN

With Jordan on the road to recovery, and my youngest two doing better after the divorce, it was time to focus on me. Since 2012, I had been toying with the idea of becoming a certified life coach and began working with a coach to help me get there. When life got in the way, that dream went on the backburner along with many other things; however, I never lost sight of that goal.

In April 2013, just before all hell broke loose in my life with Jordan's arrest, I attended a weekend seminar focused on self-help and healing that my life coach invited me to. That weekend changed my life as I was able to learn to let go of so much from my past that I was still holding on to. In the past, I never wanted to relive the hurt of my childhood abuse, which is why I never completed therapy with my counselor after the initial group sessions with Mom and my sisters. Still, those hours in that room with complete strangers forced me to examine my life in its entirety. The tears would not stop flowing and it made me so angry. I despise crying in front of anyone, *especially* people I do not know. Again, I could not stop the tears no matter what I tried. It was cleansing for my soul and the beginning of my healing journey.

That weekend I learned the process of forgiving and, ultimately, how to forgive myself. Years of shame, guilt, and torment were lifted from me. For the first time, I looked at myself in the mirror and could acknowledge all of the hurt and pain reflecting back at me in my eyes. I didn't attempt to dismiss those feelings, instead, I embraced them. With newfound courage, I vowed that I was enough and worthy of love. My heart felt light and it was as if I was born again. Those strangers became my friends as well as a new circle of support that proved to be a great help when I experienced the hurt of Jordan's arrest.

One major take away from that weekend seminar that really impacted my life was learning how to get the results I was after in life through a specific process I was taught. As a result, I wrote out my vision of being free of high blood pressure and medication. Although I was crystal clear on what I wanted to create, I wasn't sure how it would be accomplished. So many times before I wanted to be healthy and failed to follow through. This was a result of not having a proven system and adequate support to help me fulfill my desires. What I found is that amazing things happen when you are clear on what you want in life and why, as well as when you write out your goals, intentions, and an action plan to help you get there. Like magic, things began happening to move me closer to my vision. It wasn't overnight, and it wasn't easy; nevertheless, I gradually started moving towards my intended outcome.

In my single mother role, the kids and I were always at a gym between basketball practices, training sessions, or games for Jaden. Although I knew she was always incredibly fit and strong, I did not know that my little girl had amazing natural talent as a ball player. While waiting for her in the gym, I began attending group exercise classes and walking the track regularly. Fitness had been a love of mine since my middle school days when I made the cheerleading team. I knew how good exercising made me feel, but I rarely had the energy or motivation to do it consistently for any significant amount of time.

During one visit at the gym, a personal trainer started questioning me about my health and fitness. He asked my kids a question I will never forget: "Wouldn't you love to see your Mom lose weight and be healthy?" Up until that moment, my struggle with weight and health had only been personal to me. I hadn't taken time to see how it was affecting my children. Hearing their responses to him that day motivated me to look at being healthy as a benefit to us all.

When I considered everything, my weight and poor health were causing a lot of issues in multiple areas of my life. At my highest recorded weight, I was 206 pounds, and I am only 5' 2." Each month, I was going to the doctor to have my blood pressure checked because it was so hard to control. Throughout my life, I had tried pretty much every known diet on the planet with no lasting results. Up to that point, I had only been looking for a quick fix and was not willing to make a long-term commitment to doing the necessary work.

In January 2014, I committed to participating in a weight loss competition at work with three other individuals on my team. The initial weigh-in was overwhelming for me. I had been trying so hard to lose weight on my own, and went as extreme as doing juice and smoothie cleanses. Unfortunately, when I stepped on the scale that day at work, I weighed in at 200.4 pounds. In that very moment, I dedicated myself to staying in the journey no matter what. I was tired of giving up when things didn't happen as quickly as I wanted them to, or when I fell off track from whatever crazy extreme plan I was attempting to follow. This was something that had to be done, not only for me, but for my children and the sake of being healthy once and for all.

In the beginning of my journey, my life coach supported me with my initial weight loss. She pushed me and held me accountable every week. At the same time I was loving helping my co-workers and seeing them achieve results as well. Social media was another tool I used for accountability and to share my journey. I found inspiration from watching other women online who openly shared their ups and downs with fitness and nutrition. Their stories inspired me to keep going, and as a result, I wanted to pay it forward by inspiring others.

By August 2014, I became an online fitness and nutrition coach to help other women live healthier. I connected with a highly supportive community of women coaches who introduced me to new tools and programs to help in my weight loss journey. Within a year of making that commitment, my blood pressure was lowered to a normal range and my doctor cleared me of having to take blood pressure medication. I was getting stronger, losing weight, my energy was through the roof, and I was inspiring others with my journey. My dreams were once again becoming reality, and I was encouraged to set even bigger goals.

Being a certified life coach was my ultimate career choice although I had no clue when that would be made possible. I envisioned myself traveling the world, speaking before large audiences about my life, coaching others one-on-one, writing books, and creating tools to help other women who felt stuck based on their past. In the meantime though, I was still working as an Information Technology Specialist for the federal government. The pay was great and I had excellent benefits; however, internally, I was dying because I knew I wasn't living my purpose. Just the idea of walking away seemed impossible, especially with being a single parent. Besides, I had so much history there and several of my closest friends worked there as well. Even so, I knew a change was needed. Another great tip I learned from my spiritual mentor, Joyce, was to "feel the fear and do it afraid." So in the midst of my fears, I set an intention to leave my full-time, well paying, stable, comfort zone filling job with the government to pursue a career I was passionate about.

To seal the deal and hold myself accountable, I made a declaration in August 2015 through social media to the world that I would be leaving my job to become a full-time coach. A favorite saying that I quote often is, "Where focus goes, energy flows." My focus became living a life of freedom, doing what I loved to do to help others, and having time to be present in my children's lives on a daily basis.

Many circumstances and events continued to take place and served as a constant reminder of how short life truly is. The most impactful event occurred in October 2015 when my cousin Von passed away. Cancer had prematurely taken her life. Although she was in her second battle with the disease, none of us suspected that she would ever actually die from it. Before she retired from the government a few months before her passing, Von worked in the building next door to where I also worked. We would see each other there often, and of course she was still a major part of my children's lives. Von's death took a toll on my entire family and even now it is hard to believe she is gone. It happened so suddenly and left us all with a void that only her presence could fill.

Von had a passion for photography, but never pursued it full time. Instead she took great pleasure in photographing babies and members of our family whenever she had the opportunity. She captured many of the greatest memories of my children's lives as well as those of many other family members with her sophisticated camera. At any family event, we could count on Von being there to snap a million pictures. While mourning the death of my beloved cousin, I imagined what life may have been like for her had she decided to go after what she loved. I knew she got great joy from taking beautiful photographs, but I never understood why she didn't choose it as a career since she loved it so much and was naturally good at it.

A couple of months after Von's passing, I received notification from my job that I was required to travel overseas for two or more weeks for a new project I was assigned to. I felt a nudge in my spirit to take the leap. Jaden and Landen hated when I had to travel for work, which was becoming more and more frequent as my time with that agency went on. It was a big ordeal to get things in order for them to be taken care of whenever I had to travel for work, but I had been blessed to have a great support system of friends and family who always stepped in to help when I needed it most. Nevertheless, nothing in my being felt at peace about making that trip overseas.

Within six months of my declaration to the world, I turned in my three week notice and left my job of nearly seven years. I did not have a solid plan, and figuring out how I would continue to support my family beyond the money I extracted from my retirement savings was all scary; still, I took the leap of faith I felt called to take.

Chapter 9 - Jumping Isn't Easy

The starting point of all achievement is desire.

--NAPOLEON HILL

Steve Harvey played a major role in my decision to just "jump!" One day while at home, I watched a video on social media where he shared how important it is for us to jump out on faith and follow the dreams God planted in our hearts. He went on to say that when you jump, don't expect for the wind to immediately get under your wings causing you to soar. Instead, he warned that there would be many instances where you will fall down and scrape your knees, but if you stick with it, you will eventually begin to soar.

I kept Steve's words of wisdom in mind as I took my leap. Things started off great! I was doing well in my fitness and nutrition coaching and moving up in rank within the organization I was partnered with. Money was flowing steadily each week as I helped more and more people. My children were happy because I was home with them each day, and for the first time ever, we could have a summer break completely together.

As time went on, things got harder. The money I was making diminished. I went from making close to six figures at my stable job to earning less than $200 per month. My savings were depleted, bills were piling up, and fear set in. I remembered Steve Harvey's words, yet I still slipped into bouts of depression. I didn't know how I was going to feed my children, and I was on the verge of losing everything I owned, including the home I worked so hard to get. Life was scary, but I still held onto my faith. I knew God had not led me to this point to leave me or forsake me, so in spite of how I felt, I had to keep pressing forward.

I vowed to show up every day in my life and to focus on helping others instead of my circumstances. There were many times I didn't know how I would keep the lights on, but God always made a way. In the midst of this trial, I began to confess out loud daily that I was a "successful life coach, New York Times Bestselling Author, and sought-after keynote speaker." Of course, none of this was true; however, that didn't stop me from professing it on my newly established website and social media pages. I was releasing my faith and calling those things that were not as though they were.

One day while at home, I received a phone call from my eldest sister. She had seen my new website and was following me on social media. She called to inform me of a new venture she was looking into with her best friend who has been a certified life coach for many years, and she wanted to know if I would be interested in learning about becoming a certified life coach. I almost fainted from excitement while exclaiming to her that life coaching was a dream of mine since 2012, but I never was able to afford the cost of the training and certification. In that moment, she said something that cemented in my brain that God heard my cries and was giving me the desires of my heart. Her words rolled out so effortlessly, "I will pay for your training, Joy, so don't worry about that." Tears immediately filled my eyes. For all the years I struggled and worried about how I would ever make my dream a reality, God solved it in a matter of seconds through my dear, sweet sister. I know that she had no idea how much she blessed me that day. She wasn't just merely paying for training, she was investing in me, and demonstrating that she believed in me and wanted to see me be successful.

Even with this great news, it would be a few months before training could take place and I could begin earning income through coaching. My financial situation became even more desperate and I was relying on the support of friends and family to survive. God was breaking me. In my past, I relied on myself to get whatever my children or I needed and my pride would not allow me to ask others for help. This breaking process brought me to a new level of humility, and it did not feel good at all. My lowest moment was the day I had to apply for food assistance because I could not feed my children.

After experiencing being treated unkindly by people in the offices of government assistance programs in my younger years while struggling to take care of Jordan and going to school, I vowed that I would never go back to requesting government assistance again. Yet, here I was, many years later, in need of help to put food on the table. To make matters worse, it took close to two months before I received any aid. My first trip to the store ended with the cashier yelling out to me loudly, "It says your food stamp balance is zero!" while trying to pay for my groceries with my newly issued EBT card. I was humiliated and left the store in bewildering tears.

I couldn't understand how I arrived at this low point when I knew in my heart I was following the plan and vision God placed in my heart. It appeared as though I was going backwards instead of forward, but I have learned that God's plan doesn't always make sense to the human brain because His ways are not our ways. God was breaking me free from problem areas that would prevent me from being all He created me to be. There is no room for pride when living a life for God and serving His people. He was teaching me what it is like to *really* live and walk in faith so I can appreciate when He takes me to new levels. It didn't feel good, but I knew it was *producing* good for where God was leading me.

In August 2016, I became an Internationally Certified Personal Life Coach alongside my eldest sister. Due to our age difference and family history, she and I had never spent time doing anything together one-on-one. Completing our life coach training together was a significant milestone for us. Toni is my father's oldest living daughter. She was grown and lived out of state for my entire life, so there was no time for bonding or really getting to know each other. Before completing our training, we decided it was time for us to unite as real sisters to support each other as family should. Toni has played a major role in helping me to overcome the setbacks I have experienced as a result of taking my 'jump' and I am eternally grateful for her. It was in that class together with my sister that I committed to writing my first book to help other survivors of sexual abuse. God's timing is always perfect, even when we don't understand it.

When I reflect back over my life, it amazes me that I am not a complete and total basket case. Writing this book has been an emotional journey, but it has brought even more healing to my soul. Although therapy and counseling are great, it was only God's grace that ultimately saved me and brought me out. With every detour I took in life, He was right there to lead me back to the path He set before me to travel.

Throughout my life, I have faced so many negative situations that impacted my mindset and the results I was getting. This was a direct result of the sexual abuse I endured as a child; however, today I do not allow those situations to keep me from chasing after the life Jesus died for me to have. Just because I didn't get a good start in life doesn't mean that it isn't possible for me to finish strong. The same is true for you as well.

My past does not define who I am. In this moment, I am free to live life in abundance without shame or guilt for anything that has taken place in my life. That is true freedom. I'm no longer in bondage and being victimized by my circumstances. Instead, I am the creator of my destiny. Through faith and growing closer to God, my mind has been renewed. These mindset shifts have helped me get to where I am today. It didn't happen overnight, but in each trial, I gained a little more wisdom and grew a little bit closer to being the woman I was created to be.

God had a plan for me all along. Even in my darkest times, He was right there. When I felt alone it was not because He abandoned me; rather it was me who turned away from Him. In my mind, I couldn't comprehend how anyone could love me after all the mistakes and wrongs I had done. However, the truth is I didn't know how to love and accept myself. As a result, I taught others that it was okay to mistreat, disrespect, and devalue who I am. They could only do what I allowed and accepted. Even still, the choices I made didn't make Him love me any less because His love never changes.

My experiences helped to shape me into the woman I am today, and for that I am thankful. Without the struggles I endured, I wouldn't have been given three of the best blessings ever - my children. Furthermore, I wouldn't have a story to tell to inspire others like you reading this book.

Chapter 10 - The Road to Victory

Success is...knowing your purpose in life, growing to reach your maximum potential, and sowing seeds that benefit others. -- JOHN C. MAXWELL

Becoming a victor over your traumatic past all begins with your mindset. Joyce Meyer often quotes this saying, "You can be powerful or you can be pitiful, but you can't be both!" I love that quote because it is so true. Staying trapped in a negative mindset and holding on to the hurts of the past does not serve you; it only hinders you and deprives the world of experiencing your greatness.

In this chapter, I will share with you eight practical tips to help you overcome a victim mentality so you can experience victory in your life. These are tips that have helped me and I know will also help you in your journey.

Tip #1: Speak faith confessions over your life. Instead of rehearsing the limiting beliefs of your past over and over again in your mind, free yourself of those thoughts by coming up with new thoughts you can repeat daily. This is how you renew your mind! Speaking faith confessions helped me transform my thinking during my divorce, and played a major role in my daughter's transformation. When negative thoughts would enter my mind, I would speak against them by reciting a faith confession in addition to forming a habit of reciting them daily. I suggest writing your own positive affirmations that dispel the lies you have been telling yourself for years and meditating on them each day. Meditating simply means to roll a thought over and over again in your mind. For instance, instead of repeatedly telling yourself that you are worthless, confess out loud and with emotion, "I am a virtuous woman and my value is far above rubies!" Any time that old negative thought pops into your brain (and it will because you have held onto it for so long!), audibly speak against it by confessing your new belief. I personally like to base my faith confessions on the Word of God and what God says about me. What He says is true, regardless of what I have convinced myself to believe through life's experiences. When my daughter voiced her thoughts about wanting to end her life when she was in the third grade, I began teaching her and my other children to speak faith confessions. I truly believe this saved my daughter's life and helped her overcome low self esteem by embracing her individuality. When her earthly father was absent in her life, I taught her to say "God is my Father and He loves me unconditionally!" I will share my personal faith confessions with you as an appendix to this book to give you ideas on how to craft your new personal mantras. Change begins in your mind, and *then* it is manifested in your reality.

Tip #2: Invest in your personal growth daily, and IMPLEMENT what you learn. When I became a fitness and nutrition coach, I was introduced to the idea of routinely spending time in personal development as a vital behavior for success. This one behavior has transformed my life drastically. I recommend devoting a minimum of 15

- 20 minutes daily to reading books, watching videos, or listening to audiobooks, or podcasts relative to the areas you need the most support in, and then immediately put into practice what you have learned. With this information age we live in, there is no shortage of resources for accessing personal development materials to help you in every facet of life. Cost doesn't even have to be a factor with great free tools such as podcast apps, YouTube, and live broadcasting available on social media. Reading this book and implementing these tips into your life is also a great way to invest in your personal growth. The implementation of what you learn is where you will see the best results; soaking up knowledge is one thing, putting what you learned into action is entirely different. Action is the antidote to fear, and the catalyst for change!

Tip #3: Connect with your Creator! Make spending time with God a priority for each new day. Learning to connect with God each day was a habit I formed during my period of unemployment in 2009. God sustained me during that time period and continues to sustain me today as a result of me making my relationship with him a priority. Connecting with God doesn't have to be some long drawn-out process, just whatever brings you the most benefit. I like to start my day by reading a verse of scripture, reading a daily devotion of some type, and praying to God through speaking faith confessions and thanking Him for all He has done while I'm in the shower. A great tool that I use is the YouVersion Bible app on my phone. You will find many great devotionals there on a wide range of subjects, there is a new verse of the day each morning, and you can access several different translations of the Bible to make it easily understandable (I love the MSG and Amplified translations). Also, finding a spiritual mentor to learn from and listen to will often help in your spiritual growth. I, of course, love Joyce Meyer and listen to her free podcasts regularly.

Tip #4: Become a visionary! Write the vision for your life with no regard as to how farfetched it seems, or worries about how you will accomplish it. The Bible says that "without a vision, the people perish!" When you know the direction you are heading, it is much easier for you to arrive there. Your vision is your compass, God is your guide. This tip helped me when I set out to overcome obesity and high blood pressure, as well as when I decided what I wanted to ultimately do with my life. Determine what impact you will make in this world, and why your vision is important to you. Knowing why something is important to you will help you on days when you feel like giving up; so know your why and make it juicy! Write your success story with explicit details of all you will accomplish, what it will look like, who you will be surrounded by, what it will feel like, and see yourself being victorious! Be willing to hold yourself accountable and find support from others you trust who will also help to hold you accountable. Decide which action steps you know you will need to take, and take massive action every day to help you get closer to realizing your dreams. Keep your vision in front of you daily, and make no excuses for not following through with your plans. Before long, you will begin to live life on your own terms.

Tip #5: Make your health and fitness a top priority. I realized the importance of my health when I thought I was having a heart attack in 2012. It wasn't until 2014 that I actually committed to making health and fitness my lifestyle. Without your health, you are limited with what you can do. Make time for exercise and eating healthily so that you can improve the quality of your life, and increase the time you have here on earth to help others. Find support if you do not know where to begin, and do not give up no matter how long it takes to see improvements or change.

Tip #6: Learn to forgive. Forgiveness is for you; not for the other party. When you forgive, you release yourself from living in bondage. You find the freedom to move forward with your life. Forgiving those who have hurt, misused, and abused you may seem difficult at first, but it is necessary for your healing. Forgiveness does not mean that you have to remain in a relationship with those who have hurt you; instead, it means that you no longer give them power to *continue* hurting you as you move forward in life. During the weekend seminar I attended in 2013, I learned a forgiveness process that brought me so much freedom. I freed myself from so much negativity that was draining my energy by completing the following steps:

1. Make a list of every person who has ever wronged you in life.
2. Write out what they did to hurt you, and what benefit you have received by holding on to the hurt.
3. Determine what it has cost you in life to hold on to what they did to hurt you.

4. After counting the cost, release the bitterness, anger, and resentment.
5. Decide to live in peace by letting go of all the wrongs from your past, and walk in the newness of this present moment.

Tip #7: Become a cheerful giver. Focusing on helping and giving to others takes your mind off yourself. After depleting all of my savings once I took the jump to begin my entrepreneurial journey, I stayed in depression as long as my thoughts remained on all of my problems. Another quote that I love from Joyce Meyer is that in hard times you should "trust God and do good." I poured every ounce of my being into learning how to create value for others on a daily basis, and began using what I had to bless others. Helping others brings me incredible joy and leaves me with no time to feel sorry for myself. By the same token, giving places you in a position of authority and speaks volumes about who you believe you are. If you don't have money to give, give your time. Share things you have learned in your life with others. Make a difference in someone's life by just being there for them when they are facing difficult times. There are so many opportunities to give on a daily basis; seek out those opportunities by staying alert. Givers experience the most joy in life!

Tip #8: Be gentle with yourself. Change is hard and it comes in increments; not all at once. I didn't become the woman I am today without making several mistakes. As Steve Harvey said, you will fall many times before you experience victory. So be patient while you learn a new approach to living. Throughout my life I have found that it is easy to give up out of frustration, but learning to have patience and be kind to myself throughout the growing process has allowed me to see progress in many areas of my life. The world is harsh enough without us being harsher to ourselves. Things we say to ourselves we often wouldn't say to other people. Learn to forgive yourself when you make mistakes. Get back up when you fall down. Speak kindly to yourself at all times. And whatever you do, never ever give up! You too can become *VICTORIOUS*!

Appendix: Joy's Personal Faith Confessions

- I am obedient to God.
- I am a masterpiece created by God.
- I am fearfully and wonderfully made.
- I am as bold as a lion; I do not have a spirit of fear.
- I can do all things with God.
- Nothing is impossible for me.
- I love God and I love to do right at all times.
- God is the lover of my soul. He is the holder of my right hand.
- God will never leave me helpless or forsaken.
- God has an amazing plan for my life and I am blessed to be seeing it manifested right now as I speak.
- Money, wealth, health, love, joy, peace, and prosperity are all drawn to me and stick to me like glue.
- Blessings and increases chase me down everywhere I go, and every day of my life.
- I am surrounded by God's goodness, His mercy, favor, wealth and abundance; it all flows to me easily.
- I am equal to anything and ready for everything.
- I am the righteousness of God.
- I am in right standing with God.

- No weapon formed against me shall ever be able to prosper.
- I am the apple of God's eye and His greatest masterpiece; in me, He is well pleased.
- I am a cheerful giver. I love to give! And I have more than enough to give away every day of my life.
- I am a good friend and I love at all times.
- I am a virtuous woman and my value is far above rubies.
- I love to learn and I embrace wisdom.
- If anything good can happen to anybody, it can and will happen to me today! For this is the day that the Lord has made. I will rejoice and be glad in it.
- I am abundantly blessed. My home is blessed. My children are blessed. I am blessed when I come in, and I am blessed when I go out.
- I am successful. I have level 10 success in every area of my life. Everything I touch turns to gold.
- All of my bills are paid in full! I owe no man anything, but to love him.
- God is my Father and He loves me unconditionally

About the Author

Joy Regulus is an Internationally Certified Personal Life Coach, speaker, and author who specializes in helping women overcome their traumatic pasts to live the abundant, overflowing life she believes Jesus died for us all to have. As a result of her colorful life, she understands what it feels like to feel alone, depressed, overwhelmed, and defeated because she has faced many circumstances that left her feeling all of those emotions. Joy learned in her journey that her faith in God and a resolve to never give up are the keys to her reaching her overall goals.

Joy is the mother of three children, and currently resides in Huntsville, AL.

www.joyregulus.com

Cover design by Joy Regulus

Author photograph by Ronald Pollard Photography